THE NIGHT BEFORE CHRISTMAS

by
CLEMENT C. MOORE

Ideals Children's Books • Nashville, Tennessee

Copyright © 1984 by Hambleton-Hill Publishing, Inc.
All rights reserved.
Published by Ideals Children's Books
An imprint of Hambleton-Hill Publishing, Inc.
Nashville, Tennessee 37218
Printed and bound in the United States of America

ISBN 1-57102-082-9

'Twas the night before Christmas, when all through the house
Not a creature was stirring, not even a mouse.
The stockings were hung by the chimney with care
In hopes that Saint Nicholas soon would be there.

The children were nestled all snug in their beds,
While visions of sugarplums danced in their heads.
And Mama in her kerchief and I in my cap,
Had just settled down for a long winter's nap.

When out on the lawn there arose such a clatter,
I sprang from my bed to see what was the matter.
Away to the window I flew like a flash,
Tore open the shutters and threw up the sash.

The moon on the breast of the new-fallen snow
Gave a luster of midday to objects below.
When, what to my wondering eyes should appear,
But a miniature sleigh and eight tiny reindeer,
With a little old driver so lively and quick,
I knew in a moment it must be Saint Nick.

More rapid than eagles his coursers they came,
And he whistled and shouted and called them by name:
"Now, Dasher! Now, Dancer! Now, Prancer and Vixen!
On, Comet! On, Cupid! On, Donder and Blitzen!
To the top of the porch, to the top of the wall!
Now, dash away! Dash away! Dash away, all!"

As dry leaves that before the wild hurricane fly,
When they meet with an obstacle, mount to the sky,
So up to the housetop the coursers they flew
With a sleigh full of toys and Saint Nicholas too,
And then in a twinkling I heard on the roof
The prancing and pawing of each little hoof.
As I drew in my head and was turning around,
Down the chimney Saint Nicholas came with a bound.

He was dressed all in fur from his head to his foot,
And his clothes were all tarnished with ashes and soot.
A bundle of toys he had flung on his back,
And he looked like a peddler just opening his pack.
His eyes—how they twinkled! His dimples—how merry!
His cheeks were like roses, his nose like a cherry!
His droll little mouth was drawn up like a bow,
And the beard on his chin was as white as the snow.

The stump of a pipe he held tight in his teeth,
And the smoke it encircled his head like a wreath.
He had a broad face and a little round belly
That shook when he laughed like a bowl full of jelly.
He was chubby and plump, a right jolly old elf,
And I laughed when I saw him in spite of myself.
A wink of his eye and a twist of his head
Soon gave me to know I had nothing to dread.

He spoke not a word but went straight to his work,
And filled all the stockings; then turned with a jerk,
And laying his finger aside of his nose,
And giving a nod, up the chimney he rose.

He sprang to his sleigh, to his team gave a whistle,
And away they all flew like the down of a thistle.
But I heard him exclaim ere he drove out of sight,
"Happy Christmas to all and to all a good night!"

'TWAS THE NIGHT
BEFORE CHRISTMAS

(The Rest of the Story)

Paul Harvey

May I present Dr. Moore.

First, so you'll feel you know him better, let me tell you about his family.

His daddy was Benjamin Moore, a Protestant Episcopal clergyman who became a bishop in that church. His daddy was also a professor at Columbia College in New York, and in 1801 he was elected president of Columbia. And Ben's nephew became president of Columbia forty or so years later.

What I'm leading up to is that our Dr. Moore had a scholarly ancestry. It was natural that he, Clement Clarke Moore, should be born with a textbook intellect. And that Clement skipped his boyhood, grew to manhood, and nobody ever called him Clem.

Dr. Moore was a scholar. Became Professor of Biblical Learning at General Theological Seminary in New York. Learned every language but slang.

In 1809 he wrote a book. It was not exactly a best seller. Its title was *A Compendious Lexicon of the Hebrew Language.*

Then Dr. Moore became full Professor of Oriental and Greek Literature. I know he hardly sounds human. But he was. Before I'm through, you'll know he was.

In 1813 the first symptom showed up. He married. At thirty-five, the professor finally looked up from his weighty reading and his pompous writing and discovered love.

Eventually, Dr. and Mrs. Moore had children of their own. With them, for the first time in his life, the professor could descend from the intellectual stratosphere and explore with them the wonderland of make-believe.

It was one day when in play, he was thus unbending . . . that he authored a false statement. If he had just told it to his children, as any other father telling a fairy tale, nothing would have happened. But the meticulous professor had to put it in writing.

That did it. It was a story in verse about an old German handyman who worked for the Moores. The hired man was the model for the hero of this fiction. And a year later that flippant bit of writing almost cost the distinguished Dr. Moore a case of apoplexy.

Here's what happened.

Harriet Butler, daughter of the rector of St. Paul's Church in Troy, New York, was visiting. Somehow she saw that poem. She asked for a copy.

Dr. Moore may or may not have said she could have it. Certainly he expected her to respect the privacy of his little family joke. But she didn't.

She sent the poem anonymously to the *Troy Sentinel*. And the newspaper published it. Dr. Moore saw a copy of that paper. Even though his name was not printed, he hit the ceiling.

He could not write a protest to the newspaper without revealing that he, the dignified professor of Oriental languages, had authored this literary lie.

Besides, the *Sentinel's* story was quickly copied elsewhere. And repeatedly. What had been intended as a little private bedtime story was printed with no explanation and so was represented to be factual. Thousands came to believe it. By now there was nothing Dr. Moore could do but fume and fuss and hide and hope that nobody—particularly nobody among his associates at the seminary—ever found out his secret.

Actually, please understand, he had done nothing wrong. How many things we may say in play with our children which would appear pretty absurd in print.

Dr. Clement Moore managed to preserve his dignity with cautious silence for fifteen years. Then it got out.

In 1829 the *Troy Sentinel* discovered his identity. He threatened suit if they named him. Instead, the paper again printed his humorous little pretense and printed this explanation: "In response to many inquiries the *Sentinel* wished to state that this poem was written by a gentleman who belongs by birth and residence to the city of New York and that he is a gentleman of (more) merit as a scholar . . . ."

Well! That merely added to the authenticity of the thing and intensified further the public curiosity as to its source. But the doctor stood firm.

He could not let this untruth be publicly associated with his distinguished name, to bring discredit upon all his truly fine writings.

In 1837, when the *New York Book of Poetry* was published, this verse was included.

It was 1838 before he ever owned up to it. Sixteen years after it was written, fifteen years after it had been published repeatedly, when Dr. Moore's children were all grown, so they could understand what had motivated their daddy to do such a thing . . . finally he told the world *The Rest of the Story*.

He told the Troy, New York, *Budget* that he did it. That he, the Episcopal man of letters who compiled the first Hebrew dictionary in the United States, that he, the distinguished Professor of Oriental and Greek Literature, that his gifted pen had been guilty of this unmitigated deception.

And so it is that this man who wrote a verse for his children is today enshrined in the hearts of all children. On the day before Christmas there will be a pilgrimage of children . . . a lantern procession to his grave in New York's Trinity Churchyard.

For you see, Dr. Clement Clarke Moore, for all the works of which he was most proud, is remembered for the one whimsical verse which embarrassed him.

Forgotten is his *Compendious Lexicon*. Remembered is the verse which he wrote for his children.

We know best his verse which begins " 'Twas the night before Christmas . . . ."